Francis Frith's
Around Helston

Photographic Memories

Francis Frith's
Around Helston

Martin Dunning

FRITH
BOOK Co

Paperback edition first published in the United Kingdom in 2000 by
Frith Book Company Ltd

Text and Design copyright © Frith Book Company Ltd
Photographs copyright © The Francis Frith Collection

British Library Cataloguing in Publication Data

Francis Frith's Helston
Martin Dunning
ISBN 1-85937-214-7

Frith Book Company Ltd
Frith's Barn, Teffont,
Salisbury, Wiltshire SP3 5QP
Tel: +44 (0) 1722 716 376
Email: info@frithbook.co.uk
www.frithbook.co.uk

Printed and bound in Great Britain

Front Cover: Meneage Street 1913 65943

AS WITH ANY HISTORICAL DATABASE THE FRITH ARCHIVE IS CONSTANTLY BEING CORRECTED AND IMPROVED
AND THE PUBLISHERS WOULD WELCOME INFORMATION ON OMISSIONS OR INACCURACIES

Contents

Francis Frith: Victorian Pioneer   7

Frith's Archive - A Unique Legacy   *10*

Around Helston - an Introduction   *12*

Helston   *16*

East of Helston   *45*

West of Helston   *54*

The Lizard   *69*

Index   *87*

Free Mounted Print Voucher   *91*

Francis Frith: *Victorian Pioneer*

FRANCIS FRITH, Victorian founder of the world-famous photographic archive, was a complex and multi-talented man. A devout Quaker and a highly successful Victorian businessman, he was both philosophic by nature and pioneering in outlook.

By 1855 Francis Frith had already established a wholesale grocery business in Liverpool, and sold it for the astonishing sum of £200,000, which is the equivalent today of over £15,000,000. Now a multi-millionaire, he was able to indulge his passion for travel. As a child he had pored over travel books written by early explorers, and his fancy and imagination had been stirred by family holidays to the sublime mountain regions of Wales and Scotland. 'What a land of spirit-stirring and enriching scenes and places!' he had written. He was to return to these scenes of grandeur in later years to 'recapture the thousands of vivid and tender memories', but with a different purpose. Now in his thirties, and captivated by the new science of photography, Frith set out on a series of pioneering journeys to the Nile regions that occupied him from 1856 until 1860.

Intrigue and Adventure

He took with him on his travels a specially-designed wicker carriage that acted as both dark-room and sleeping chamber. These far-flung journeys were packed with intrigue and adventure. In his life story, written when he was sixty-three, Frith tells of being held captive by bandits, and of fighting 'an awful midnight battle to the very point of surrender with a deadly pack of hungry, wild dogs'. Sporting flowing Arab costume, Frith arrived at Akaba by camel seventy years before Lawrence, where he encountered 'desert princes and rival sheikhs, blazing with jewel-hilted swords'.

During these extraordinary adventures he was assiduously exploring the desert regions bordering the Nile and patiently recording the antiquities and peoples with his camera. He was the first photographer to venture beyond the sixth cataract. Africa was still the mysterious 'Dark Continent', and Stanley and Livingstone's historic meeting was a decade into the future. The conditions for picture taking confound belief. He laboured for hours in his wicker dark-room in the sweltering heat of the desert, while the volatile chemicals fizzed dangerously in their trays. Often he was forced to work in remote tombs and caves where conditions were cooler. Back in London he exhibited his photographs and was 'rapturously cheered' by members of the Royal Society. His reputation as a photographer was made overnight. An eminent modern historian has likened their impact on the population of the time to that on our own generation of the first photographs taken on the surface of the moon.

Venture of a Life-Time

Characteristically, Frith quickly spotted the opportunity to create a new business as a specialist publisher of photographs. He lived in an era of immense and sometimes violent change. For the poor in the early part of Victoria's reign work was a drudge and the hours long, and people had precious little free time to enjoy themselves. Most had no transport other than a cart or gig at their disposal, and had not travelled far beyond the

boundaries of their own town or village. However, by the 1870s, the railways had threaded their way across the country, and Bank Holidays and half-day Saturdays had been made obligatory by Act of Parliament. All of a sudden the ordinary working man and his family were able to enjoy days out and see a little more of the world.

With characteristic business acumen, Francis Frith foresaw that these new tourists would enjoy having souvenirs to commemorate their days out. In 1860 he married Mary Ann Rosling and set out with the intention of photographing every city, town and village in Britain. For the next thirty years he travelled the country by train and by pony and trap, producing fine photographs of seaside resorts and beauty spots that were keenly bought by millions of Victorians. These prints were painstakingly pasted into family albums and pored over during the dark nights of winter, rekindling precious memories of summer excursions.

The Rise of Frith & Co

Frith's studio was soon supplying retail shops all over the country. To meet the demand he gathered about him a small team of photographers, and published the work of independent artist-photographers of the calibre of Roger Fenton and Francis Bedford. In order to gain some understanding of the scale of Frith's business one only has to look at the catalogue issued by Frith & Co in 1886: it runs to some 670 pages, listing not only many thousands of views of the British Isles but also many photographs of most European countries, and China, Japan, the USA and

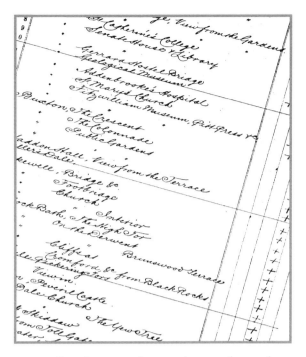

Canada – note the sample page shown above from the hand-written *Frith & Co* ledgers detailing pictures taken. By 1890 Frith had created the greatest specialist photographic publishing company in the world, with over 2,000 outlets – more than the combined number that Boots and W H Smith have today! The picture on the right shows the *Frith & Co* display board at Ingleton in the Yorkshire Dales. Beautifully constructed with mahogany frame and gilt inserts, it could display up to a dozen local scenes.

Postcard Bonanza

The ever-popular holiday postcard we know today took many years to develop. In 1870 the Post Office issued the first plain cards, with a pre-printed stamp on one face. In 1894 they allowed other publishers' cards to be sent through the mail with an attached adhesive halfpenny stamp. Demand grew rapidly, and in 1895 a new size of postcard was permitted called the court card, but there was little room for illustration. In 1899, a year after Frith's death, a new card measuring 5.5 x 3.5 inches became the standard format, but it was not until 1902 that the divided back came into being, with address and message on one face and a full-size illustration on the other. *Frith & Co* were in the vanguard of postcard development, and Frith's sons Eustace and Cyril continued their father's monumental task, expanding the number of views offered to the public and recording more and more places in Britain, as the coasts and countryside were opened up to mass travel.

Francis Frith died in 1898 at his villa in Cannes, his great project still growing. The archive he created continued in business for another seventy years. By 1970 it contained over a third of a million pictures of 7,000 cities, towns and villages. The massive photographic record Frith has left to us stands as a living monument to a special and very remarkable man.

Frith's Archive: *A Unique Legacy*

FRANCIS FRITH'S legacy to us today is of immense significance and value, for the magnificent archive of evocative photographs he created provides a unique record of change in 7,000 cities, towns and villages throughout Britain over a century and more. Frith and his fellow studio photographers revisited locations many times down the years to update their views, compiling for us an enthralling and colourful pageant of British life and character.

We tend to think of Frith's sepia views of Britain as nostalgic, for most of us use them to conjure up memories of places in our own lives with which we have family associations. It often makes us forget that to Francis Frith they were records of daily life as it was actually being lived in the cities, towns and villages of his day. The Victorian age was one of great and often bewildering change for ordinary people, and though the pictures evoke an impression of slower times, life was as busy and hectic as it is today.

We are fortunate that Frith was a photographer of the people, dedicated to recording the minutiae of everyday life. For it is this sheer wealth of visual data, the painstaking chronicle of changes in dress, transport, street layouts, buildings, housing, engineering and landscape that captivates us so much today. His remarkable images offer us a powerful link with the past and with the lives of our ancestors.

Today's Technology

Computers have now made it possible for Frith's many thousands of images to be accessed almost instantly. In the Frith archive today, each photograph is carefully 'digitised' then stored on a CD Rom. Frith archivists can locate a single photograph amongst thousands within seconds. Views can be catalogued and sorted under a variety of categories of place and content to the immediate benefit of researchers.

Inexpensive reference prints can be created for them at the touch of a mouse button, and a wide range of books and other printed materials assembled and published for a wider, more general readership - in the next twelve months over a hundred Frith local history titles will be published! The day-to-day workings of the archive are very different from how they were in Francis Frith's time: imagine the herculean task of sorting through eleven tons of glass negatives as Frith had to do to locate a particular

See Frith at www. frithbook.co.uk

sequence of pictures! Yet the archive still prides itself on maintaining the same high standards of excellence laid down by Francis Frith, including the painstaking cataloguing and indexing of every view.

It is curious to reflect on how the internet now allows researchers in America and elsewhere greater instant access to the archive than Frith himself ever enjoyed. Many thousands of individual views can be called up on screen within seconds on one of the Frith internet sites, enabling people living continents away to revisit the streets of their ancestral home town, or view places in Britain where they have enjoyed holidays. Many overseas researchers welcome the chance to view special theme selections, such as transport, sports, costume and ancient monuments.

We are certain that Francis Frith would have heartily approved of these modern developments in imaging techniques, for he himself was always working at the very limits of Victorian photographic technology.

The Value of the Archive Today

Because of the benefits brought by the computer, Frith's images are increasingly studied by social historians, by researchers into genealogy and ancestory, by architects, town planners, and by teachers and schoolchildren involved in local history projects.

In addition, the archive offers every one of us an opportunity to examine the places where we and our families have lived and worked down the years. Highly successful in Frith's own era, the archive is now, a century and more on, entering a new phase of popularity.

The Past in Tune with the Future

Historians consider the Francis Frith Collection to be of prime national importance. It is the only archive of its kind remaining in private ownership and has been valued at a million pounds. However, this figure is now rapidly increasing as digital technology enables more and more people around the world to enjoy its benefits.

Francis Frith's archive is now housed in an historic timber barn in the beautiful village of Teffont in Wiltshire. Its founder would not recognize the archive office as it is today. In place of the many thousands of dusty boxes containing glass plate negatives and an all-pervading odour of photographic chemicals, there are now ranks of computer screens. He would be amazed to watch his images travelling round the world at unimaginable speeds through network and internet lines.

The archive's future is both bright and exciting. Francis Frith, with his unshakeable belief in making photographs available to the greatest number of people, would undoubtedly approve of what is being done today with his lifetime's work. His photographs, depicting our shared past, are now bringing pleasure and enlightenment to millions around the world a century and more after his death.

Around Helston - *An Introduction*

HUNDREDS OF YEARS ago, a fiery dragon flew over the little Cornish town of Helston, dropping a large stone in what is now Angel Yard and frightening the population out of their wits. However, no-one was hurt and the people celebrated their narrow escape by dancing in and out of each other's houses; the stone was eventually used in the building of the Angel Hotel. So runs the legend of the origins of Helston's famous Furry Dance, held each year on 8 May. In fact, the ceremony dates back to pre-Christian times, when many Cornish settlements would have greeted the arrival of summer with a fertility ritual which involved dancing and the bringing of flowers and greenery into the town from the woods outside. The early Christians - presumably working on the principle of 'if you can't beat 'em, join 'em' - subsumed this pagan ritual into their religion, and it is surely no accident that Flora Day is celebrated on the Feast of the Apparition of St Michael, the patron saint of the parish.

The Celtic Christians were early settlers of the area around Helston, but there had been settlements here for thousands of years. To the west of the town, on a hillside near Crasken, is a prehistoric settlement, while the hills of Carnmenellis to the north and the plateau of the Lizard to the south have standing stones, burial grounds and earthworks aplenty. The climate was agreeable (if a little damp), the valleys of the Cober and Helford rivers provided fish and wildfowl, and the plateau of the Lizard was a good hunting ground. And one day someone, somewhere, discovered that the granite hills to the north and west held tin. Silver-white, easily worked and smelted, tin was to become the lifeblood of the county, boosted by the Bronze

Age's demand for the metal which, when combined with copper, made durable weapons and utensils. Tin was traded far and wide, and even before the Romans arrived, links had been forged with Europe and distant civilisations like the Phoenicians.

When the Celtic Christian missionaries and monks started to arrive from Brittany and Ireland in the 5th and 6th centuries, they found fertile ground in which to sow the seeds of their faith. Their names are preserved in place names such as Mullion (Melanus) and Breage (Breaca), and in church dedications like St Winwalloe, while the remote area to the south of the Helford River is still known as Meneage from the Cornish Meneghek, or 'monks' land'. Helston's name is thought to come from the Celtic Henlys, meaning 'Old Court', an indication that it was a settlement of some importance, perhaps a Celtic capital; by the turn of the first millennium it had become the royal manor of Henlyston, held by Edward the Confessor and subsequently King Harold. With the Norman invasion of 1066 it passed into the hands of William the Conqueror, and the Domesday Book of 1086 records 4,760 acres ploughed by 20-40 teams of oxen, along with various breweries and mills.

Helston was becoming an important market town and transport centre. Its farming hinterland provided all sorts of produce, and it was the junction of several land routes. Occupying as it does a site between the natural barriers of the Cober and Helford Rivers, it was the gateway to the Lizard to the south, while to the north and west roads led to the mining areas in the hills. North-east lay the growing port of Truro, and westwards were Penzance and the monastery on St Michael's Mount.

Most importantly, Helston was the best port to the west of the Lizard. Mount's Bay is exposed during southerly storms; while little harbours such as Porthleven provided a modicum of shelter, the only port to provide safety, and the one that was closest to the source of the tin, was Helston. It is difficult to imagine today that the neatly-mown grass of the bowling green was until the 14th century the estuary of the Cober, once bustling with ships loading tin, leather, and all the commodities that make a busy little market town tick. There was a castle - built by the Earl of Cornwall - and St John's Priory Hospital, built to care for the many travellers that passed through.

King John recognised and enhanced Helston's status in 1201 when he granted the town its first charter, making it only the second town in Cornwall, after Launceston, to become a free borough. The charter grandly proclaims that ' ... our burgesses of the same town shall have a gild merchant, and quittance throughout our whole land from toll, pontage, passage, stallage, lastage, and soilage'.

Despite Royal recognition and a flourishing

trade, all was not well; the forces of nature were to deal the town a drastic blow. Atlantic swells pushed up by the prevailing south-westerly winds, combined with the action of tides and currents, were moving huge quantities of sand and shingle inexorably eastwards around Mount's Bay. Navigating the mouth of the Cober became increasingly difficult as sandbars grew and shifted, and in 1302 Helston was finally cut off from the sea for ever when the Loe Bar closed the entrance; it formed Loe Pool, which according to legend is the place where Arthur threw Excalibur. Another legend is that the bar was formed when the giant Tregeagle, chased by the devil, dropped a bag of sand in the river mouth. The blocking of the Cober may have been bad news for Helston, but it was the making of Gweek. Four miles to the east of the town, and at the head of the tidal estuary of the Helford River, Gweek now took on the role of Helston's port, a part it was to play until the early 20th century.

In spite of being now landlocked, Helston continued to flourish and grow. It received a succession of royal charters - including Edward III's of 1336, which granted a Saturday market and four fairs a year - and became a stannary town. The Stannaries were the hubs of the Cornish economy, charged with assaying, stamping and recording the production of tin so that the King could more effectively raise duties and taxes. The twice-yearly coinage fairs were equivalent to the

farmers' cattle markets: mine owners would bring their metal to the Coinage Hall for weighing and valuing, and for three or four days a carnival atmosphere would prevail in the town, aided, no doubt, by copious draughts of Spingo at the Blue Anchor opposite the Coinage Hall.

Tin was vitally important - the mines employed thousands directly, and thousands more in the service industries - and the midsummer coinage session of 1595 recorded 110,000 pounds weight of tin, nearly fifty tons. Little wonder, then, that mine owners such as Sir Francis Godolphin grew fantastically wealthy, or that on the back of this success, a whole new professional class of lawyers, solicitors and bankers should spring up. Cross Street is the manifestation in bricks and mortar of their power, a street of early banks and grand houses such as Lismore, home of the Grylls family, and the Ratcliffe's Penhellis House.

Methodist and Baptist chapels were built to compete for the souls of the faithful with the parish church of St Michael, and Helston Grammar School, known as the Eton of Cornwall, educated the sons of the wealthy. Municipal buildings were erected; the Guildhall, the ultimate symbol of civic pride, was built in 1839, and on the darker side of human affairs the old Borough Prison was built on Shute Street in 1837. In 1838 the coinage system was abandoned, but the miners carried on producing tin, and the quarrymen of Constantine and Tregonning Hill

dug yet more granite to be used in the building of splendid edifices such as the new Methodist Chapel and Godolphin Hall.

Mining's star began to wane in the early 20th century, and today only one mine is (just) working - South Crofty near Camborne. Porthleven's fishing fleet, along with that of Mullion, declined when fish stocks crashed and mechanisation and intensive farming reduced the workforce employed in agriculture. Through all these changes, however, one thing remained constant - the Furry Dance. It had its ups and downs - in 1875 it was recorded that only 16 couples danced - but it has remained Helston's very own celebration of the summer, unique apart from the 'Obby 'Oss at Padstow.

The 8am Hal-an-Tow ceremony, with adults and children carrying branches and singing 'Summer is a come O, and Winter is a gone O' is an echo of the earliest Pagan rituals. The children's dance at 10am is a relatively new addition, first danced in 1922 and the only dance to be celebrated through the dark days of World War Two. The principal dance is at midday, when men in top hats and tails and women in formal gowns weave in and out of shops, houses and gardens accompanied by the Helston Town Band and cheered on by the thousands of onlookers who come from all corners to join the festivities and admire the unchanged beauty of this fine Cornish town.

Helston

*Coinagehall Street
1903* 49591

General View 1890 24495
This photograph was taken from the south,
probably somewhere near what is now the
cemetery at Whitehill. On the far left, in the valley of
the River Cober, lies St Johns, and on the horizon
are Prospidnick Hill (slightly right of centre) and
Trannack Downs (right).

◀ **General View c1955**
H69058
The dilapidated roof in the foreground, reminiscent in its undulating way of the Old Post Office at Tintagel, is probably that of a barn. The state of the roof is an interesting counter to the argument that 'they don't build things like they used to' - cowboy builders have flourished since time began.

◀ From Bullock Lane 1895 36184

The land immediately to the right of St Michael's Church, a field only five years before, is now built up. The bulky building just right of centre is the former Baptist Chapel on Wendron Street, which became a furniture showroom in 1902 and the Flora Cinema in 1914. The curtain came down for the last time in 1985.

▼ From Porthleven Road c1950 H69041

This picture was probably taken just down the road from Penventon Farm. The big house set back from the road left of centre is Weeth, and past it the road continues down into the valley of the Cober.

◀ St John's Hill 1913 65938

St Johns occupies the opposite bank of the Cober on the road (once a turnpike) to Penzance. It was here, in the late 18th century, that John Wesley built a Methodist Chapel. He could not build one in Helston itself owing to the locals' antipathy to Methodism, which meant that a preacher could not walk through the town without getting stoned.

The Moors 1890 24503
The Moors is the rough, open valley floor to the north-west of Helston, popular for walks, trysts and blackberrying. Clearly visible is the raised leat which took water to the corn mill in the town.

On the Stream c1870 5638
The stream is actually the River Cober, which used to regularly flood this area of Lower Green. When this happened, bands of men were despatched to Loe Bar to dig a channel to drain off the floodwater, and the Corporation, in accordance with custom, presented the Lord of the Manor with a leather purse containing three halfpennies. Today a permanent culvert prevents flooding.

The Lake 1913 65946
This is an odd echo of the past; moored hereabouts 700 years ago would have been ocean-going trading vessels loading up with tin. The inexorable growth of the Loe Bar at the mouth of the Cober gradually made navigation more difficult, and in 1302 Helston was finally cut off from the sea.

The Lake 1913 65945
We are looking north-east up the valley to the town. St Michael's is on the skyline, and round the bend in the valley to the left is the site of St John's Priory Hospital, which cared for travellers and lepers from 1220 to 1580.

The Lake 1922 73271
The lake was created as part of Coronation Park, which turned what had previously been a patch of soggy wasteland into a public pleasure ground to commemorate the coronation of George V in 1911.

The Park c1950 H69035
In the foreground is the A394, which leads right to Breage and Penzance and left to Penryn and Falmouth. Between the road and the lake is the site of the cattle market.

Coronation Park c1955 H69087
It is a pleasant summer afternoon in the park, judging from the woman's dress and the flowers in bloom. The balmy climate of the south-west allows all sorts of plants to flourish, including tropical species such as the palms and bamboo seen here. And how do boys make go-karts today, now that pram wheels like these are no longer available?

The Park c1955 H69099
The fifties were a more innocent time - today no sensible boat owner would leave the rowlocks on an unattended boat for fear they would be stolen. The fine stand of trees that once occupied the island, visible in picture No 65945, have been felled and replaced with shrubs.

▼ **The Tennis Courts, Coronation Park c1955** H69074
Wooden racquets (good old Dunlop Maxply, by the look of it) and
plimsolls. A far cry from today's carbon fibre, and there's not a Nike,
Reebok or Adidas logo to be seen anywhere.

▼ **View from the Park c1955** H69053
We are looking up Monument Road towards the back of Coinagehall
Street. On the skyline is the Methodist Chapel, built in 1888 at a cost of
£5,000. In 1988 the building was declared unsafe; it was refurbished,
and re-opened in 1995 after £360,000 had been spent on it.

▲ **The Monument 1890**
24502
The inscription reads 'To
the memory of Humphrey
Millett Grylls'. The Grylls
were prominent burghers
of the town in the 18th
and 19th centuries, and
lived at Bosahan on the
Helford River. They had
something of a monopoly
on the mayorship of
Helston - four members
of the family held the
post a total of 23 times!

◀ **The Monument 1895** 36190
Humphrey Millett Grylls (1789-
1834) was idolised in the town after
he managed to save the Wheal Vor
mine, three miles away near
Sithney, and the 1,200 jobs it
provided. The monument, built by
local mason Thomas Eva, was
erected on Grylls' death in 1834.

The Grylls Monument c1950 H69039
Buried at the south-west corner of the monument, written on vellum and then put in a bottle, is the Latin eulogy written for Humphrey Millett Grylls by the Rev Derwent Coleridge, son of the poet who wrote 'The Rime of the Ancient Mariner'.

The Monument and the Bowling Green 1922 73270
Helston's Bowling Club was founded in 1760, and the green was laid in 1764. It is one of the oldest in the country - but not as old as that on Plymouth Hoe, which was in use as early as 1588 when Drake played his famous game there.

The Bowling Green c1955 H69069
This was once the site of Helston Castle, built in the 13th century by Edmund, Earl of Cornwall. Despite its apparent weaknesses - it was built on low-lying ground surrounded by hills - it commanded the head of the estuary. With the cutting-off of the Cober the castle lost its raison d'etre, and it was in ruins by the late 15th century.

Coinagehall Street c1955 H69067
The Coinage Hall stood in the middle of the street. From 1243 until 1546 the site was occupied by the Chapel of Our Lady, but at the Reformation it was incorporated into the row of buildings which included the Coinage Hall, the Duchy Officer's house and the gaol.

Coinagehall Street c1955 H69092

The Coinage Hall was the scene of the twice-yearly coinage sessions, when mine owners brought their tin into town for assay and auction. The term coinage derives from the French 'coin', meaning corner - a piece of the ingot would be cut from the corner for assaying.

Coinagehall Street c1955 H69081

On the left, just down from the bank, is the Guildhall, which was built in 1839 on the site of the old market house. On Flora Day it is decorated with greenery; it is the starting point for the midday Furry Dance, which was traditionally the preserve of the gentry.

◀ **Coinagehall Street c1955** H69033
On Flora Day (held on or near 8 May) this lower section of Coinagehall Street is busy with dancers and stalls, decorated with flags and thronged with onlookers. Flora Day has not always thrived like it does today - in 1875 it is recorded that only 16 couples danced.

◀ Coinagehall Street
1903 H69501

The Godolphins built the Angel as their town house in the 17th century, and it became a hotel in the mid 18th century. It has long been at the centre of life in Helston, having functioned as gaol, excise house and tax office, as well as hosting the more usual functions such as balls and meetings.

▼ The Post Office c1955
H69082

The ugly Post Office (right) replaced the fine old granite building which was once the town house of the Trevenen family of Bonython Manor. The Trevenen's House later became Simpson's Garage, visible next to the Central Restaurant in picture No 73267.

◀ Coinagehall Street
1931 84215

What was the Cornish Bank (designed by W J Winn, who also built the Methodist Chapel) is now Lloyd's. Just out of the picture on the left stands Barclay's, once the home of Hugh Rogers, who was the first Squire of Penrose.

**Coinagehall Street
1913** 65941
Great Western Railway
motor buses like the
one struggling up the
hill past the Cornish
Bank were introduced
in 1903, but it was
many years before the
horse disappeared from
the streets. On the left
Martin and Son,
Wholesale and Retail
Grocers are making a
delivery by horse cart.

◄ **Coinagehall Street 1913** 65940
In 1910 the Mayor announced from the Guildhall steps that as a mark of respect for the late King Edward VII the Furry Dance was to be postponed. In 1886 it was actually cancelled following the deaths of two prominent townswomen, Mrs Trevenen and Miss Grylls. Wakehams the Chemists are still trading today.

Coinagehall Street 1922 73267

At the bottom of the street on the left, hidden in this view behind the Methodist Chapel, is the famous Blue Anchor Inn. It has what is believed to be the oldest private brewery in the country; the brewery produces Spingo, a pale beer which comes in three strengths, the strongest of which can make even hardened drinkers a trifle wobbly.

Cross Street 1914 66702

The building on the left with the iron balcony is Great Office, where local mine accounts were handled; it was once the Register Office. On the right are the gardens of Lismore, home of the Grylls family. The pump, dating from 1844, is still there.

The Parish Church 1895 36191

The church has an unusual east window designed by Krugar Gray in 1938 which depicts two angels dancing the Furry Dance. The huge 24-branch brass chandelier was donated by the earl of Godolphin during rebuilding.

The Church, South-West 1890 24500
St Michael's Church (dedicated to the town's patron saint) was built between 1756 and 1761 by the 2nd earl of
Godolphin and designed by the Greenwich architect Thomas Edwards. It replaced the old church, which had
become so decrepit (owing to a lightning strike and a subsequent fire) that services were being held in the Guildhall.

The Parish Church c1950 H69040

The fine 103ft tower has a peal of eight bells. The church is built with granite from Tregonning Hill near Breage;
granite is notoriously difficult to work, and this accounts for the relative lack of decoration of many Cornish churches.

The Church 1913 65944

The Church 1913
The churchyard contains the grave of Henry Trengrouse, inventor of the rocket apparatus used by lifeboats and the coastguard to fire rescue lines onto ships in distress. Much affected by witnessing the wreck of the 'Anson' in 1807, Trengrouse came up with the idea after watching the fireworks on the Lower Green that celebrated George III's birthday.

The Market House 1895
Godolphin Hall was built in 1888 on the site of Helston Grammar School, which had stood there from 1835, when the headmaster was Rev Derwent Coleridge, son of the poet. Since 1976 it has been the home of the Godolphin club.

The Market House 1895 36193

Wendron Street 1913 65942
This wonderful picture (although almost certainly posed!) looks down towards the crossroads at the Guildhall. Opposite Godolphin Hall is the former Baptist Chapel, which became the Flora Cinema at about this time.

Wendron Street c1950 H69046
Spot the differences from picture No 65942. The beautiful row of thatched cottages has gone, to be replaced by a rather uninspiring three-gabled house, and uphill from it there is what appears to be a garage. There is not a horse in sight.

Wendron Street 1906
55249
In 1863 the boxer Bob Fitzsimmons was born in a thatched cottage at the top of Wendron Street. Prior to Lennox Lewis, he was the last Englishman to win the World Heavyweight Boxing Championship when he defeated Jim Corbett in 1897.

▼ **Wendron Street c1955** H69079
Here we see another example of how the passage of time changes the face of a street. The pavements have been straightened out and the road metalled, and Read and Roberts has become the Montdore Ladies Salon. There is also considerably more advertising.

▼ **Meneage Street 1895** 36187
We are looking down towards the Cornish Bank on the corner of Wendron Street and Church Street, with plenty of Victoriana on show. Above the horse and cart is a penny-farthing bicycle shop sign, while the lad in the road on the left rests on his hoop.

▲ **Meneage Street 1913**
65943
On the left is the Bell Inn, thought to originate from the early 18th century, and just down the road is the Rodney. It was originally called the Admiral Boscawen after a maritime hero; the name was changed to the Lord Rodney in 1780, when he won a famous battle against the Spanish at Cape St Vincent.

◀ **Meneage Street 1924**
76617
The water channels between pavement and road, so characteristic of Helston's streets, are known as kennels, probably derived from the Cornish word 'gannel'; this in turn is a corruption of the English 'channel'. It makes you wonder why they didn't just stick with the original word.

Meneage Street 1931 84219

This view is very similar to picture No 76617 - even down to the convertible with its hood up parked outside Carlyon's newsagents - but there are one or two subtle changes. The road surface is vastly improved, and Courtney Wearne the jewellers has gone - along with its clock, which had been there for at least forty years.

Meneage Street c1955 H69089

Here we have a tale of two breweries: the Devenish Brewery (a Cornish concern despite its name) fell victim to recession in the 1980s, while the St Austell Brewery flourishes still, long after its founding by Walter Hicks. Its most potent brew is Hicks Special Draught, also known by its nickname of High Speed Death.

East of Helston

Gweek, The River c1960 G73019
Lying at the very head of the tidal estuary of the Helford River,
Gweek was for centuries Helston's port, and the old quay area can
be seen by the group of buildings on the left. Gweek was also a
centre for smuggling and piracy, and in the 14th century Helston
merchants had a gallows erected here to deter would-be offenders
and punish actual ones.

**Gweek, The Village
1904** 53046
This scene shows a
very different world
from ours today: the
visit of the boot repairer
to the village. The sign
reads 'Courtis Bespoke
Repairs, noted for Hob
Boots', one pair of
which, complete with
nails, probably weighed
five time as much as a
pair of trainers.

◄ **Gweek, The Village and the Stream c1950**
G73008
The harbour, run by the Gweek Company, was in past centuries busy with ships from Holland, Ireland, Germany and Scandinavia, loading and discharging cargoes of coal, timber, grain and stone. The Helston Customs House was also here, but it moved to Helford in 1822.

◄ **Gweek, The Village Green 1904** 53045
The wheeled contraption on the right is probably a log cart. Imported logs were stored in a pool before being taken inland, often to the mines. For particularly big logs, five or six horses had to be used; the carters would leave Gweek at 5am, sometimes returning as late as 9 or 10pm - a long day, for which they would receive the princely sum of 2s 6d.

▼ **Gweek, The Post Office and the Village c1960** G73021
Here we see almost the same view as picture No 53046, but how things have changed. Telegraph poles, road signs and the car indicate the communication revolution. There is also a plethora of tobacco advertising - Capstan, Craven 'A', Players and Senior Service - which would not be seen today.

◄ **Gweek, The Bridge Shop c1950** G73013
Livestock in a Cornish village is not unusual, but Gweek now has some rather unusual mammalian residents. Just down the river is the internationally famous seal sanctuary, founded in the 1950s by midlander Ken Jones to take care of sick, injured or orphaned seals.

Gweek, The Lodge c1960 G73304
This lodge, with its pillared porch and thatched roof, was built to a design common on the Trelowarren estate - the gamekeeper's cottage is very similar. The dormer window was in 1895 a little gable, proving that things change more than appearances might suggest.

Constantine, Polwheveral Creek c1955 C408011
Polwheveral Creek opens into the wide estuary of the Helford River just south of Lower Calamansack, where Sir Arthur Quiller-Couch based his poem 'Helford River'.

Constantine, Polwheveral Creek c1955 C408010
The remote creeks of the Helford River were not always so wooded - many of the trees were planted in the 18th century to provide fuel for the tin smelters. Scott's Quay on Polwheveral Creek was the main shipping point for Constantine stone, and as late as 1935 there were still eight quarry companies working in the parish.

Constantine, Lower Fore Street c1955 C408013
Constantine's fine terraces are built with granite dug from one of the many quarries nearby, which also furnished the stone for Waterloo Bridge. There were also several mines, including Wheal Vyvyan, Wheal Caroline and East Wheal Rose, at which, in the 18th century, miners earned £3 a month.

▼ **Constantine, The Old Town c1950** C408003
Constantine once had a Cornish Arms (just round the corner to the right) and a Queens Arms, but in 1929 they both came under the same ownership; the Queens Arms was closed, and the name was transferred to the Cornish Arms. The cottage by the telegraph pole is Mole Cottage.

▼ **Constantine, The Post Office c1950** C408002
The local lads were once known as 'Pilchard Tails': in accordance with the Lizard saying that 'it is no sin to rob the government', they were much involved in piracy and smuggling. A reward of £300, offered in 1828 for the capture of those who assaulted two customs officers, was never claimed because everybody was involved in the trade.

▲ **Constantine
The Village c1950**
C408001
In 1963 Constantine was the scene of the murder of William Rowe, a reclusive farmer. He deserted from the army in World War One, and was hidden by his family until an amnesty was declared after World War Two. His killers were after his fortune, but they never found it - he had concealed it in jam jars hidden in a hedge.

◀ **Kennack Bay c1950**

H69023

Kennack Sands is a popular spot for an afternoon on the beach. Legend has it that in the 17th century the pirate Captain Avery buried 12 boxes of gold here; but despite many searches, they have never been found. The rocks in the distance are Carrick Luz ('Grey Rock') and the farthest headland is Black Head.

West of Helston

Praa Sands, General View 1927 79968
This popular holiday spot, with its mile of fine
beach, has grown considerably since 1927. The
headland on the left is Hoe Point. Just beyond it is
Prussia Cove, home in the 18th century of the
smuggler John Carter, known as the 'King of
Prussia', who carried out his activities on a grand
scale and even mounted a battery of guns to deter
the Revenue men.

Praa Sands, General View 1930 83115
In the foreground is Pengersick Castle, a fortified manor from the early 16th century; it has a 62-step granite spiral staircase, and is now listed as an ancient monument. The field on the right is now Pengersick caravan site.

Praa Sands, The Camping Ground c1955 P109034
Caravanning in the fifties was a rather more rudimentary affair than it is today, although in its way probably no less enjoyable. In place of hurricane lamps, primus stoves and chemical toilets, today's big trailers have mains electricity, running hot and cold water and flush toilets - and not quite the same sense of adventure.

Breage, The Queen's Arms c1955 B491008
The 15th-century Queen's Arms is still the centre of village life. Just up the road on the right is Breage House, once the home of the local squire but now, like so many big old houses, a residential home.

Breage, Pelor Road c1955 B491005
On the left is the tower of the Church of St Breaca, a 6th-century Irish missionary who was unusual in being female. The church was built in 1466, and was the place of worship of the Godolphin family from nearby Godolphin Hall. It has some very rare 15th-century wall paintings.

Helston, Godolphin Hall 1895 36194
The Godolphins were prominent in the affairs of Helston until the line died out with the 2nd earl in the late 18th century. The name lives on in the Godolphin racing stable (ironically owned by Sheikh Makhtoum); it is named after Godolphin Arabian, one of the three Arab stallions from which all British racehorses are descended, and imported by the 2nd earl.

Porthleven, The Harbour and the Lookout 1890 24509
Porthleven's large fishing fleet caught mackerel and crabs, but its most important quarry was pilchards. One catch in November 1834 was 2,000 hogsheads (108,000 gallons!) and by 1880 there were 85 pilchard boats operating. The total fleet was 144 boats, employing nearly 600 men and boys.

Porthleven, The Harbour and Tregonning Mill 1924 76631
The harbour was completed in 1858, with the flood gate (visible in the centre) raised for the first time on 7 October. The gate was intended to stop storm surges wrecking the fleet, but it was also used to allow flushing of tin waste from the Great Wheal Vor Mine which would otherwise have silted up the harbour.

**Porthleven
The Harbour 1890**
24513
On the left is St Bartholomew's Church, consecrated in 1842, and on the right the Methodist Chapel. Like most fishing communities, Porthleven's fleet did not usually work on Sundays, although not everybody went to church - the 'Good Templars' did their duty, while the 'Good Tipplers' stayed at home and enjoyed other pleasures.

**Porthleven
The Harbour and Bay
View Terrace 1924**
76630
On windy days, when putting to sea was difficult, teams of men would tow boats out to the end of the pier, or the skipper could pay 1s a time for the job to be done by horse. It is likely that none of the men in this picture could swim, and their heavy boots and clothing meant that going overboard would have only one outcome.

**Porthleven
Fore Street 1931**

84223

The village's heyday was from 1870-90; after that the introduction of engines reduced the crew needed and catches fell, and by the early 20th century boatbuilding and supporting industries were beginning to tail off. The population, which had been as high as 2,400 in 1883, fell to 1,600 by 1912.

◄ **Porthleven**
Fore Street 1935 86576
In the background is the Methodist Chapel, the third to be built in Porthleven. The foundations were laid on 8 June 1881, and the chapel was opened on 11 May 1883; it was built from granite, with Delabole and Bangor slate for the roof. The total cost was £3,700, and the architect was James Hicks of Redruth.

◀ **Porthleven**
Breage Side 1924 76627
Centre right is the Ship Inn, and on the left the Lifeboat House. Porthleven's first lifeboat, in 1863, was the 'Agar Robartes', which was replaced in 1882 by the 'Charles Henry White'. The Lifeboat House was built in 1893 at a cost of £1,400; in 1900 the 'John Francis White' was stationed here, followed in 1926 by the 'Dash'. The station closed in 1929.

 **Helston, Loe Pool**
1890 24506
More correctly known as the Loe (meaning 'pool' in Cornish), this mile-long freshwater lake was formed in the 13th century when the River Cober became dammed by a sand and shingle bar - Loe Bar. Today it is owned by the National Trust.

◀ **Helston, Loe Pool**
1890 24504
In 1837 the local squire, Reverend Canon Rogers, commissioned James Rendell to design a harbour for the Loe. The plan, which would have involved breaching the Loe Bar and running a canal inland all the way to Helston, was priced at £118,523; not surprisingly, it was never carried out.

Helston
Penrose Walk 1913

Penrose Walk runs from the bottom end of Coronation Park down to the Loe and follows its shore to Penrose. The Rogers family gave 1600 acres of their estate, including the Loe, to the National Trust in 1974 - at that time the single biggest gift the Trust had received.

Helston
Penrose from the Park 1890

The Rogers family, Squires of Penrose, have provided a long line of MPs, JPs, solicitors and lawyers. Hugh Rogers bought the Manor of Penrose in 1770 from the Penrose family, who had owned it since the 13th century.

Helston, Penrose Walk 1913 65947

Helston, Penrose from the Park 1890 24508

Gunwalloe, The Bay and the Poldhu Hotel 1899 43811
Poldhu means 'Blackpool' in Cornish, but there is little resemblance between this wild headland and its northern namesake - save for the hotel. It was built as a result of the Victorian railway boom, and occupies a site similar to that of the Headland Hotel at Newquay. It is now a residential home.

Mullion, The Golf Links 1911 64022
'A good walk spoiled' was how Oscar Wilde described golf, but no doubt these Edwardian gentlemen would disagree. The man putting is probably guilty of the most hideous sartorial faux pas in that he is not wearing a hat. In the background is the Poldhu Hotel.

Mullion, The Poldhu Hotel 1904 52256
The four large masts in the background were part of the Marconi Wireless Telegraphic Station; they were erected in 1902. Public interest in the emerging radio technology was high, and the Prince of Wales and his wife visited the station in 1903.

Mullion, The Marconi Memorial 1939 88946
The memorial commemorates the first radio signal sent across the Atlantic on 12 December 1901. The Morse letter 'S' was transmitted here to St John's, Newfoundland, where Guglielmo Marconi was eagerly listening. The Poldhu station closed in 1937, and the memorial was erected in the same year.

Mullion, From the Caves 1890 24254
The rugged coast of the Lizard has, over the centuries, supported many forms of maritime enterprise, among them
smuggling; caves such as these provided a handy hideaway for both smugglers and contraband.

Mullion, Fishermen 1924 76638
Mullion's harbour was not built until 1887, and before that the west-facing cove was dangerously exposed. Even a small swell could make launching hazardous, and during storms boats had to be dragged well up the beach out of reach of the waves.

◀ **Mullion**
The Quayside c1955
M107007
In March 1867 the Dutch ship 'Jonkheer Meester van der Wall van Putteshoek', carrying spices, sugar and coffee, was wrecked on Men-y-Grib during a storm. Only one man survived out of a crew of 26; the bodies were laid out on the quayside before being taken up the hill to be buried in the churchyard.

**Mullion
The Harbour 1939**
88943
By this time the rowing gigs and sailing luggers were being replaced by boats with engines, some of which can be seen pulled up on the slipway. On the right, the harbour wall has been badly damaged by a storm; it was not fully repaired until after the war.

Mullion, The Village 1904 52261
Mullion takes its name from St Melaine, the 6th-century Bishop of Rennes, who excommunicated two British priests who went to preach on his patch. St Mellion, at the other end of the county, is also named after him.

**Mullion
The Village 1904** 52266
There is another explanation of Mullion's name - it was at one time called Porth Mellin, 'the cove of the mill', and a mill existed here until the 19th century. The village itself lies a mile north-east of the cove.

Mullion, The Old Inn 1904 52268
The Old Inn is one of Mullion's best-known buildings. In 1904 the
landlord was Orlando Bosustow; before him the licence was held by
Miss Mary Mundy, whose teas were apparently 'worthy of the gods'.
The wall and building on the left are now no more.

Goonhilly, The GPO Satellite Station c1960 G184005
Following in Marconi's footsteps, the (then) GPO built their satellite station here on the open downs at Goonhilly (in Cornish 'Gunhelgy', meaning hunting down) 300 feet above sea level. The main dish (nowadays supplemented by several others) is 85 feet across and weighs 800 tons.

Frith Book Co Titles

www.frithbook.co.uk

The Frith Book Company publishes over 100 new titles each year. A selection of those currently available are listed below. For latest catalogue please contact Frith Book Co.

Town Books 96pp, 100 photos. County and Themed Books 128pp, 150 photos (unless specified). All titles hardback laminated case and jacket except those indicated pb (paperback)

Around Bakewell	1-85937-113-2	£12.99		Around Great Yarmouth	1-85937-085-3	£12.99
Around Barnstaple	1-85937-084-5	£12.99		Around Guildford	1-85937-117-5	£12.99
Around Bath	1-85937-097-7	£12.99		Hampshire	1-85937-064-0	£14.99
Berkshire (pb)	1-85937-191-4	£9.99		Around Harrogate	1-85937-112-4	£12.99
Around Blackpool	1-85937-049-7	£12.99		Around Horsham	1-85937-127-2	£12.99
Around Bognor Regis	1-85937-055-1	£12.99		Around Ipswich	1-85937-133-7	£12.99
Around Bournemouth	1-85937-067-5	£12.99		Ireland (pb)	1-85937-181-7	£9.99
Brighton (pb)	1-85937-192-2	£8.99		Isle of Man	1-85937-065-9	£14.99
British Life A Century Ago	1-85937-103-5	£17.99		Isle of Wight	1-85937-114-0	£14.99
Buckinghamshire (pb)	1-85937-200-7	£9.99		Kent (pb)	1-85937-189-2	£9.99
Around Cambridge	1-85937-092-6	£12.99		Around Leicester	1-85937-073-x	£12.99
Cambridgeshire	1-85937-086-1	£14.99		Leicestershire (pb)	1-85937-185-x	£9.99
Canals and Waterways	1-85937-129-9	£17.99		Around Lincoln	1-85937-111-6	£12.99
Cheshire	1-85937-045-4	£14.99		Lincolnshire	1-85937-135-3	£14.99
Around Chester	1-85937-090-x	£12.99		London (pb)	1-85937-183-3	£9.99
Around Chichester	1-85937-089-6	£12.99		Around Maidstone	1-85937-056-x	£12.99
Churches of Berkshire	1-85937-170-1	£17.99		New Forest	1-85937-128-0	£14.99
Churches of Dorset	1-85937-172-8	£17.99		Around Newark	1-85937-105-1	£12.99
Colchester (pb)	1-85937-188-4	£8.99		Around Newquay	1-85937-140-x	£12.99
Cornwall	1-85937-054-3	£14.99		North Devon Coast	1-85937-146-9	£14.99
Cumbria	1-85937-101-9	£14.99		Northumberland and Tyne & Wear		
Dartmoor	1-85937-145-0	£14.99			1-85937-072-1	£14.99
Around Derby	1-85937-046-2	£12.99		Norwich (pb)	1-85937-194-9	£8.99
Derbyshire (pb)	1-85937-196-5	£9.99		Around Nottingham	1-85937-060-8	£12.99
Devon	1-85937-052-7	£14.99		Nottinghamshire (pb)	1-85937-187-6	£9.99
Dorset	1-85937-075-6	£14.99		Around Oxford	1-85937-096-9	£12.99
Dorset Coast	1-85937-062-4	£14.99		Oxfordshire	1-85937-076-4	£14.99
Down the Severn	1-85937-118-3	£14.99		Peak District	1-85937-100-0	£14.99
Down the Thames	1-85937-121-3	£14.99		Around Penzance	1-85937-069-1	£12.99
Around Dublin	1-85937-058-6	£12.99		Around Plymouth	1-85937-119-1	£12.99
East Sussex	1-85937-130-2	£14.99		Around St Ives	1-85937-068-3	£12.99
Around Eastbourne	1-85937-061-6	£12.99		Around Scarborough	1-85937-104-3	£12.99
Edinburgh (pb)	1-85937-193-0	£8.99		Scotland (pb)	1-85937-182-5	£9.99
English Castles	1-85937-078-0	£14.99		Scottish Castles	1-85937-077-2	£14.99
Essex	1-85937-082-9	£14.99		Around Sevenoaks and Tonbridge		
Around Exeter	1-85937-126-4	£12.99			1-85937-057-8	£12.99
Exmoor	1-85937-132-9	£14.99		Around Southampton	1-85937 088-8	£12.99
Around Falmouth	1-85937-066-7	£12.99		Around Southport	1-85937-106-x	£12.99

Available from your local bookshop or from the publisher

Frith Book Co Titles (continued)

Scottish Castles	1-85937-077-2	£14.99		Around Torbay	1-85937-063-2	£12.99
Around Sevenoaks and Tonbridge	1-85937-057-8	£12.99		Around Truro	1-85937-147-7	£12.99
Around Southampton	1-85937-088-8	£12.99		Victorian & Edwardian Kent	1-85937-149-3	£14.99
Around Southport	1-85937-106-x	£12.99		Victorian & Edwardian Maritime Album		
Around Shrewsbury	1-85937-110-8	£12.99			1-85937-144-2	£17.99
Shropshire	1-85937-083-7	£14.99		Victorian & Edwardian Yorkshire	1-85937-154-x	£14.99
South Devon Coast	1-85937-107-8	£14.99		Victorian Seaside	1-85937-159-0	£17.99
South Devon Living Memories	1-85937-168-x	£14.99		Warwickshire (pb)	1-85937-203-1	£9.99
Staffordshire (96pp)	1-85937-047-0	£12.99		Welsh Castles	1-85937-120-5	£14.99
Stone Circles & Ancient Monuments				West Midlands	1-85937-109-4	£14.99
	1-85937-143-4	£17.99		West Sussex	1-85937-148-5	£14.99
Around Stratford upon Avon	1-85937-098-5	£12.99		Wiltshire	1-85937-053-5	£14.99
Sussex (pb)	1-85937-184-1	£9.99		Around Winchester	1-85937-139-6	£12.99

Frith Book Co titles available Autumn 2000

Cotswolds (pb)	1-85937-230-9	£9.99	Sep		English Country Houses	1-85937-161-2	£17.99	Oct
Cornish Coast	1-85937-163-9	£14.99	Sep		Folkestone (pb)	1-85937-124-8	£9.99	Oct
County Durham	1-85937-123-x	£14.99	Sep		Humberside	1-85937-215-5	£14.99	Oct
Dorset Living Memories	1-85937-210-4	£14.99	Sep		Manchester (pb)	1-85937-198-1	£9.99	Oct
Dublin (pb)	1-85937-231-7	£9.99	Sep		Norfolk Living Memories	1-85937-217-1	£14.99	Oct
Herefordshire	1-85937-174-4	£14.99	Sep		Preston (pb)	1-85937-212-0	£9.99	Oct
Kent Living Memories	1-85937-125-6	£14.99	Sep		Reading (pb)	1-85937-238-4	£9.99	Oct
Leeds (pb)	1-85937-202-3	£9.99	Sep		Salisbury (pb)	1-85937-239-2	£9.99	Oct
Ludlow (pb)	1-85937-176-0	£9.99	Sep		South Hams	1-85937-220-1	£14.99	Oct
Norfolk (pb)	1-85937-195-7	£9.99	Sep		Suffolk (pb)	1-85937-221-x	£9.99	Oct
North Yorks (pb)	1-85937-236-8	£9.99	Sep		Swansea (pb)	1-85937-167-1	£9.99	Oct
Somerset	1-85937-153-1	£14.99	Sep		West Yorkshire (pb)	1-85937-201-5	£9.99	Oct
Surrey (pb)	1-85937-240-6	£9.99	Sep					
Tees Valley & Cleveland	1-85937-211-2	£14.99	Sep		Around Aylesbury (pb)	1-85937-227-9	£9.99	Nov
Thanet (pb)	1-85937-116-7	£9.99	Sep		Around Bradford (pb)	1-85937-204-x	£9.99	Nov
Tiverton (pb)	1-85937-178-7	£9.99	Sep		Around Chichester (pb)	1-85937-228-7	£9.99	Nov
Victorian and Edwardian Sussex					East Anglia (pb)	1-85937-265-1	£9.99	Nov
	1-85937-157-4	£14.99	Sep		East London	1-85937-080-2	£14.99	Nov
Weymouth (pb)	1-85937-209-0	£9.99	Sep		Gloucestershire	1-85937-102-7	£14.99	Nov
Worcestershire	1-85937-152-3	£14.99	Sep		Greater Manchester (pb)	1-85937-266-x	£9.99	Nov
Yorkshire Living Memories	1-85937-166-3	£14.99	Sep		Hastings & Bexhill (pb)	1-85937-131-0	£9.99	Nov
					Helston (pb)	1-85937-214-7	£9.99	Nov
British Life A Century Ago (pb)					Lancaster, Morecombe & Heysham (pb)			
	1-85937-213-9	£9.99	Oct			1-85937-233-3	£9.99	Nov
Camberley (pb)	1-85937-222-8	£9.99	Oct		Peterborough (pb)	1-85937-219-8	£9.99	Nov
Cardiff (pb)	1-85937-093-4	£9.99	Oct		Piers	1-85937-237-6	£17.99	Nov
Carmarthenshire	1-85937-216-3	£14.99	Oct		Wiltshire Living Memories	1-85937-245-7	£14.99	Nov
Cheltenham (pb)	1-85937-095-0	£9.99	Oct		Windmills & Watermills	1-85937-242-2	£17.99	Nov
Cornwall (pb)	1-85937-229-5	£9.99	Oct		York (pb)	1-85937-199-x	£9.99	Nov

See Frith books on the internet www.frithbook.co.uk

FRITH PRODUCTS & SERVICES

Francis Frith would doubtless be pleased to know that the pioneering publishing venture he started in 1860 still continues today. A hundred and forty years later, The Francis Frith Collection continues in the same innovative tradition and is now one of the foremost publishers of vintage photographs in the world. Some of the current activities include:

Interior Decoration

Today Frith's photographs can be seen framed and as giant wall murals in thousands of pubs, restaurants, hotels, banks, retail stores and other public buildings throughout the country. In every case they enhance the unique local atmosphere of the places they depict and provide reminders of gentler days in an increasingly busy and frenetic world.

Product Promotions

Frith products are used by many major companies to promote the sales of their own products or to reinforce their own history and heritage. Frith promotions have been used by Hovis bread, Courage beers, Scots Porage Oats, Colman's mustard, Cadbury's foods, Mellow Birds coffee, Dunhill pipe tobacco, Guinness, and Bulmer's Cider.

Genealogy and Family History

As the interest in family history and roots grows world-wide, more and more people are turning to Frith's photographs of Great Britain for images of the towns, villages and streets where their ancestors lived; and, of course, photographs of the churches and chapels where their ancestors were christened, married and buried are an essential part of every genealogy tree and family album.

Frith Products

All Frith photographs are available Framed or just as Mounted Prints and Posters (size 23 x 16 inches). These may be ordered from the address below. From time to time other products - Address Books, Calendars, Table Mats, etc - are available.

The Internet

Already twenty thousand Frith photographs can be viewed and purchased on the internet. By the end of the year 2000 some 60,000 Frith photographs will be available on the internet. The number of sites is constantly expanding, each focussing on different products and services from the Collection.
The main Frith sites are listed below.

www.francisfrith.co.uk
www.frithbook.co.uk

See the complete list of Frith Books at:

www.frithbook.co.uk

This web site is regularly updated with the latest list of publications from the Frith Book Company. If you wish to buy books relating to another part of the country that your local bookshop does not stock, you may purchase on-line.

For further information, trade, or author enquiries please contact us at the address below:
The Francis Frith Collection, Frith's Barn, Teffont, Salisbury, Wiltshire, England SP3 5QP.
Tel: +44 (0)1722 716 376 Fax: ⌐44 (0)1722 716 881 Email: uksales@francisfrith.com

---

See Frith books on the internet www.frithbook.co.uk

TO RECEIVE YOUR FREE MOUNTED PRINT

Mounted Print
Overall size 14 x 11 inches

Cut out this Voucher and return it with your remittance for £1.50 to cover postage and handling, to UK addresses. For overseas addresses please include £4.00 post and handling. Choose any photograph included in this book. Your SEPIA print will be A4 in size, and mounted in a cream mount with burgundy rule lines, overall size 14 x 11 inches.

Order additional Mounted Prints at HALF PRICE (only £7.49 each*)

If there are further pictures you would like to order, possibly as gifts for friends and family, purchase them at half price (no additional postage and handling required).

Have your Mounted Prints framed*

For an additional £14.95 per print you can have your chosen Mounted Print framed in an elegant polished wood and gilt moulding, overall size 16 x 13 inches (no additional postage and handling required).

---

* IMPORTANT!
These special prices are only available if ordered using the original voucher on this page (no copies permitted) and at the same time as your free Mounted Print, for delivery to the same address

---

Frith Collectors' Guild

From time to time we publish a magazine of news and stories about Frith photographs and further special offers of Frith products. If you would like 12 months FREE membership, please return this form.

Send completed forms to:
The Francis Frith Collection, Frith's Barn, Teffont, Salisbury, Wiltshire SP3 5QP

Voucher for FREE and Reduced Price Frith Prints

Picture no.	Page number	Qty	Mounted @ £7.49	Framed + £14.95	Total Cost
		1	**Free of charge***	£	£
			£7.49	£	£
			£7.49	£	£
			£7.49	£	£
			£7.49	£	£
			£7.49	£	£

Please allow 28 days for delivery	*** Post & handling**	**£1.50**
Book Title	**Total Order Cost**	**£**

Please do not photocopy this voucher. Only the original is valid, so please cut it out and return it to us.

I enclose a cheque / postal order for £ . . . .
made payable to 'The Francis Frith Collection'
OR please debit my Mastercard / Visa / Switch / Amex card
(credit cards please on all overseas orders)

Number . . . .

Issue No(Switch only) . . . . . . .Valid from (Amex/Switch) . . . .

Expires . . . . Signature . . . .

Name Mr/Mrs/Ms . . . .

Address . . . .

. . . .

. . . .

. . . . Postcode . . . .

Daytime Tel No . . . . Valid to 31/12/02

The Francis Frith Collectors' Guild

Please enrol me as a member for 12 months free of charge.

Name Mr/Mrs/Ms . . . .

Address . . . .

. . . .

. . . .

. . . . Postcode . . . .